YOU ARE NOT ABANDONED

A 30-Day Daily Devotional on Anxiety

Chloe Schaffer

Contents

Introduction

Our world is filled with so much negativity, which takes its toll on us from time to time and in various degrees. This explains why anxiety would sometimes fasten itself on us, sowing thoughts of doubt and loneliness in our minds. This explains those days you woke up feeling neglected, abandoned, purposeless, and without direction for life. It explains the moments you wonder if God knows you or is aware of your existence. It describes those moments you doubt if God hears you when you pray. Understand that these thoughts and feelings aren't exactly yours, and they also aren't peculiar to you. They're the negativities of this world rubbing off on you. Finally, however, we have good news!

JOHN 16:33

I have told you these things, so that in me you may have peace. In this world you will have trouble. But take heart! I have overcome the world.

The Lord is aware of and has addressed our situation. His will for us is that we live a life of peace in Him, irrespective of the negativities in our world. He has, for our sakes, overcome the world and all its negativities. The New American Standard Bible (NASB) renders the latter part of the scripture above thus: "*...take courage; I have overcome the world.*" In other words, what we've got to do is to draw courage from the fact that Jesus Christ has overcome the world for us. We have to take His Words for it. In learning and meditating on the fact that He has overcome the world for us, we can "take courage."

This devotional journal provides you with sufficient resources to "take courage," It encapsulates God's words of comfort, exhortation, inspiration, and encouragement for you in just thirty daily devotional articles. In reading through and carefully and following through every article, you'll be exposed to insights, wisdom, and instructions that will help you break free from anxiety and enjoy a life of peace in Christ. In addition, each day's article features short prayers/affirmations, further studies, and "my resolution" segments to aid your daily study.

It is my prayer that this devotional journal meets you at the points of your needs. I pray that you would find, within it, nuggets and encounters that will transform you and help you live a life of peace, joy, and fulfilment in Christ.

Day 1: He does the caring

1 Peter 5:7

Cast all your anxiety on him because he cares for you.

I am blessed with two beautiful kids, Craig and Sharon, who are both in their mid-teens today. One of the several interesting things I observed, watching them grow, is their complete dependence and trust in their parents. It never bothered them when they wanted or needed anything at all—they simply communicated it to their parents (I and my husband) and went about their business believing it was done. Isn't this how God wants us to cast all our cares on Him?

Craig and Sharon's trust in their parents indeed always paid off (and still does). This is because my husband and I (their parents) know what they need and are perhaps more passionate about providing for them than they desire to get their needs. They didn't have to worry about how we would go about meeting those needs. They trust that we love them and would go out of our way, if needs be, to ensure that their needs are met. We do the caring for them. All they need do is trust us.

Similarly, God expects us to trust and cast all our cares on Him. He expects us to believe that He can go ahead to fix things up for us. After all, He is aware of our needs even before we ask Him (Matthew 6:8).

Like Craig and Sharon would cast their cares on their parents without any worry in their minds, God expects us to cast all our cares on Him without doubt or anxiety. He sure cares for us and would work things out for our good. He is passionate about delivering you from trouble and helping you live that fulfilling life you desire.

PRAYER

I cast all my cares on the Lord. I refuse to be burdened with worry, fear, and anxiety. I trust in God's ability to guide me and deliver me from trouble and confusion. Hence, I walk in the peace of the Lord, living the glorious life that He has provided for me, in Jesus' name.

FURTHER STUDY
Philippians 4:5-9, Matthew 6:28-34

MY RESOLUTION
-

_____

_____

_____

Day 2: You Have a Father Who Hears You

1 John 5:14

This is the confidence we have in approaching God: that if we ask anything according to his will, he hears us.

In His sermon on the mount, Jesus, speaking, brings to the notice of his hearers that, despite being evil and mere imperfect humans, they care to give good things to their children. He said this to present the picture of God as the ideal father (or parent) to them: *If you, though you are evil, know how to give good gifts to your children, how much more will your Father in heaven give good gifts to those who ask him!* (Matthew 7:11)

In other words, God is much more a responsible and caring parent to us than we are or can ever be to our children. If you would go out of your way to ensure the well-being of your children, then know that God will do much more for you. God is that father our souls long for. We have to be conscious of His availability and care for us. We have to bear in mind that He always hears us every time we approach Him in prayer.

God wants us to know that He listens to us and hears us. He wants us to come to Him in prayer and fellowship with the awareness that He always hears us. So today, do well to embrace the practice of praying with the confidence that your heavenly father hears you.

PRAYER

In Jesus' name, I walk in the consciousness that I have a Father who always hear me. I refuse to allow doubt and anxiety lord it over me. As I pray today, I pray in faith and in expectation that God hears and responds to me.

FUTHER STUDY

John 14:13-14. John 15:7, 16

MY RESOLUTION

_____

_____

_____

Day 3: He Never Leaves You

Matthew 28:20

...And surely I am with you always, to the very end of the age

Have you ever felt like you are alone with your troubles? Has it ever seemed like no one understands your plight or like no one can address your particular challenges? Well, feelings like these aren't peculiar to you. Without the consciousness of the Lord's presence with us, such thoughts may infiltrate our minds often. But, they are all a façade. The eternal and unwavering reality is that the Lord would never leave us. He said it Himself: I am with you always.

David understood this reality, and he assured his son, Solomon, of it. David also said to Solomon his son, "Be strong and courageous, and do the work. Do not be afraid or discouraged, for the LORD God, my God, is with you. He will not fail you or forsake you... (1 Chronicles 28:20) He knew the Lord would never forsake His own and assured His son of this truth so passionately. The Lord has not changed. He is the same. Jesus Christ lucidly assures us of this with His words, I will not leave you as orphans; I will come to you. (John 14:18).

With the understanding and consciousness that the Lord would not abandon you, you can bask in His love and compassion for you. You can take advantage of the comfort and encouragement that His presence brings. You can also walk in His leading and let Him guide you in your daily affairs.

PRAYER

Henceforth, I walk in the consciousness that the Lord would not leave nor forsake me. I refuse to succumb to thoughts of loneliness and depression, in Jesus' name.

FURTHER STUDY
Psalm 37:25. Hebrews 13:5

MY RESOLUTION

_____

_____

_____

Day 4: God Wants the Best for You

Jeremiah 29:11

For I know the plans I have for you, declares the Lord, plans to prosper you and not to harm you, plans to give you hope and a future.

One of the significant causes of anxiety today is the uncertainty of the future. The thought that anything negative can happen to you at any time and alter the course of your life may sometimes flood your mind. The news of the negativities in our world may take its toll on you, draining your trust and hope for a brighter future. But God has different news for you. He has a plan for you. He intends to give you a brighter future.

You and I aren't forsaken in this world. We have a father who cares for us and has a great plan for our future. His plans are never to harm us, but to protect and guide us. David was well aware of this fact when he excitedly declared, Surely your goodness and love will follow me all the days of my life... (Psalm 23:6) We too can declare the same!

We all desire that our children, students, followers, fans, or protégées trust us. Right? God, our heavenly Father, requires the same of us. He wants us to take His words for it and believe that He indeed has our future effectively taken care of. This is what you and I have to do—we have to believe that our heavenly Father wants the best for us and has a great future in store for us.

PRAYER

I walk in sync with God's plans for my life. I refuse to succumb to confusing thoughts about my future. I trust in His abilities to take me from where I am to where I am supposed to be, in Jesus' name.

FURTHER STUDY

Joshua 1:1-9. Psalm 4:5

MY RESOLUTION

-

_____

_____

_____

Day 5: He is Your Sure Refuge and Fortress

Psalms 91:2-6

I will say of the LORD, "He is my refuge and my fortress, my God, in whom I trust." Surely he will save you from the fowler's snare and from the deadly pestilence. He will cover you with his feathers, and under his wings you will find refuge; his faithfulness will be your shield and rampart. You will not fear the terror of night, nor the arrow that flies by day, nor the pestilence that stalks in the darkness, nor the plague that destroys at midday.

A refuge is a safe shelter or accommodation, especially one which protects or shields one from external violence. A fortress can be described as a heavily protected place (i.e. a military base). Now, these words are used to describe the role of our heavenly Father in our lives. The Psalmist here is unequivocally declaring that the Lord is a fortified base for us. This means we are safe under His watch!

The description of the Lord as a refuge and a fortress to us also features within it responsibilities that we should take. The first verse of Psalm 91 (from which the text above is taken) is instructive: *Whoever dwells in the shelter of the Most High will rest in the shadow of the Almighty* (Psalm 91:1). We have to consciously dwell in the "shelter" of the Most High by putting our trust in Him and living in and by His Word. His Words are the strategies and secrets He provides us to enable us to live victoriously in this world.

PRAYER

Henceforth, I choose to consciously abide in the secret place of the Most High by my devotion to His Word. I put His Word to work in my daily affairs, with faith in my heart. I remain steadfast in my trust and faith in His faithfulness, in Jesus' name.

FURTHER STUDY

Psalm 91:1-16. Proverbs 3:24-25

MY RESOLUTION

_____

_____

_____

Day 6: God is Not Mad at You

Isaiah 54:10

Though the mountains be shaken and the hills be removed, yet my unfailing love for you will not be shaken nor my covenant of peace be removed, says the LORD, who has compassion on you.

Sometimes, when you err, sin, or fall short of the moral standards expected of you, it is normal to feel remorseful. Remorse is the feeling we get when we do something we know we shouldn't do or compromise on our spiritual or moral convictions. As a child of God (one who acknowledges, worships, and is devoted to Him), we shouldn't resist feeling remorseful when we do something wrong—it is a feeling that expresses our inward repentance. Instead, we should resolve in our hearts to consciously get better.

While it is okay to feel remorseful, it is essential to avoid pushing it to the extreme. A lot of times, there can be a thin line between remorse and anxiety. There were times I allowed remorseful feelings to crystalize into feelings of guilt, fear or uncertainty about God's love for me. Perhaps, you sometimes feel the same way too. That feeling that God is out to punish and hurt you for your wrong (whether or not you've repented of your sin) is a façade.

The Apostle Paul, writing to the Roman church, expresses our inseparableness from God's love: *Who shall separate us from the love of Christ? Shall trouble or hardship or persecution or famine or nakedness or danger or sword?* (Romans 8:35). Isn't this just what God says in the opening text quoted above this article? *...my unfailing love for you will not be shaken nor my covenant of peace be removed* (Isaiah 54:10).

PRAYER

I walk in the consciousness of God's unwavering love for me. I am inspired unto good works by His unwavering love, in Jesus' name.

FURTHER STUDY

Romans 8:35-39. Psalm 86:15

MY RESOLUTION

_____

_____

_____

Day 7: His Word is Your Sure Guide

Psalm 119:105

Your word is a lamp for my feet, and a light on my path

When Joshua took over the baton to lead the people of Israel from Moses, God appeared to him and instructed him on how he could be successfully guided through his life's journey. The nitty-gritty of these instructions to Joshua was the need for him to be attentive to God's Word. So God told him: *Keep this Book of the Law always on your lips; meditate on it day and night, so that you may be careful to do everything written in it. Then you will be prosperous and successful* (Joshua 1:8).

In a world that makes it seem like you are alone and without any source of inspiration or guidance, understand that God consistently leads and offers you guidance through His Word. In other words, you should not walk in confusion or despair because God's Word provides you with instructions and comfort.

When it seems like we are failing or without success in our endeavours, we can look up to God's Word for inspiration. In his letter to Timothy, the Apostle Paul, echoing God's instruction to Joshua, says: *Meditate on these things; give yourself entirely to them, that your progress may be evident to all* (1Timothy 4:15 NKJV). The lesson here is that God's Word is a sure guide for our success in life. We can live productively, successfully, and joyfully through the guidance that God's Word offers us.

PRAYER

God's Word is my sure guide. Therefore, I choose to attend to it every day of my life. I cease to be distracted from devotion to His Word, and I walk in the wisdom and inspiration that I find in it, in Jesus' name.

FURTHER STUDY
Proverbs 4:20-23. Psalm 119:130

MY RESOLUTION

_____

_____

_____

Day 8: You Can Effect Changes in Your Life

John 16:24

...Ask and you will receive, and your joy will be complete

One of the major fuels of anxiety and confusion is feeling overwhelmed by your problems and challenges. It is the feeling that there is nothing you can do to effect desired changes in your situation. But these feelings often rob you of your ability to exercise your God-given authority in any area of your life—your health, family, relationships, and financial/material wellbeing. You can ask and receive and effect your desired changes!

Jesus lets us see that we have the right to use His name in prayers concerning situations where we desire changes. He said: *And whatever you ask in My name, that I will do, that the Father may be glorified in the Son* (John 14:13). Isn't this just wonderful!

Perhaps, Peter and John understood this when they worked a miracle at the temple gate called Beautiful (Acts 3:1-8). They were going into the temple to pray when they saw a lame man begging for alms. Looking at the lame man, Peter said: *...Silver or gold I do not have, but I give you what I do have. In the name of Jesus Christ of Nazareth, walk* (Acts 3:6). As a result, the lame man received strength, walked, jumped, praising God (Acts 3:8). This happened because the Apostle Peter chose to use the authority in the name of Jesus. You can do the same today!

FURTHER STUDY
Luke 10:19. John 15:7, 16

MY RESOLUTION

_____

_____

_____

Day 9: Set Your Mind on God's Word

Proverbs 4:23

Above all else, guard your heart, for everything you do flows out from it.

You must have observed by experience that the information you allow into your mind at any given moment would determine how you feel and behave at that moment. So, for instance, how we would react to a piece of good news isn't the same way we would respond to some not-so-good news.

In the same vein, some seemingly inconsequential information allowed into the mind may, in the long run, play essential roles in our lives and determine how we would feel and behave in future. This is why the scriptures teach us to "guard our heart (or mind)." This means being careful about the information we allow inside our minds.

Thoughts of fear and anxiety are products of the information we have allowed into our minds over time. Understand that fear, panic, doubt, anxiety, etc., do not spring up from anything; they spring from the information we have allowed in our minds consciously or unconsciously. This is why the scriptures teach us to *...not conform to the pattern of this world but be transformed by the renewing of your mind* (Romans 12:2).

Indeed, the way to live joyfully and victoriously in life is to guard our hearts. The things we eventually do are the results of the information we allow into our minds. This means that when we allow only positive information into our minds, we would think and act only positively and often feel positive. With only positive input in our minds, we create positive energy in and around us.

PRAYER

My mind is sanctified. Only positive and godly thoughts are allowed in it. I refuse to be yield to negative information and thoughts. I stay joyful, hopeful, strong, and healthy, in Jesus' name.

FURTHER STUDY

Proverbs 4:20-2. Psalm 1:1-3

MY RESOLUTION

_____

_____

_____

Day 10: Get Your Thinking Right

Philippians 4:8

Finally, brothers and sisters, whatever is true, whatever is noble, whatever is right, whatever is pure, whatever is admirable—if anything is excellent or praiseworthy—think about such things

The text above obviously presents God's instructions for how we ought to guide our minds. It simply asks us to take hold of the thoughts we allow in our minds by taking the thinking action. This means avoiding any information or thought that doesn't conform to the standards listed: whatever is true, noble, right, pure, admirable, excellent or praiseworthy. In other words, whatever thoughts you and I must embrace should be one that meets these standards.

One way to do this is to constantly examine the content of the thoughts that infiltrate our minds and carry out a mental, environmental clean-up. This means consciously getting rid of ideas that do not conform to standards by replacing them with thoughts that do. It means ensuring that we are constantly thinking about true, noble, right, pure, admirable, excellent, and praiseworthy things.

You may say, Well, I am unable to come-up with something positive to think about at the moment. Well, the Bible gives us a clue on how to do this. The epistle to the Colossian church instructs, *Let the word of Christ dwell in you richly...* (Colossians 3:16 NKJV). You can do just this by thinking about the good news of the message of Christ. Instead of thinking about your fears and challenges, for instance, you can consider the privilege to pray and have your prayers answered. Just redirect your thoughts by replacing negative thoughts with the exciting news of God's word.

PRAYER

I choose to focus my attention on only things that are true, noble, right, pure, admirable, excellent, and praiseworthy. I refuse to accommodate thoughts of fear and uncertainty.

FURTHER STUDY

2Timothy 2:15-16. 1Timothy 4:15-16

MY RESOLUTION

_____

_____

_____

Day 11: The Joy of the Lord is Your Strength

Nehemiah 8:10

Go and enjoy choice food and sweet drinks, and send some of those who have nothing prepared. This day is holy to our Lord. Do not grieve, for the joy of the Lord is your strength.

The background to the text above is fascinating. Here, the children of Israel were mourning and weeping, having just heard the words of the Lord read out to them (verse 9). They hadn't been living uprightly and were pricked by their conscience at the words read to them.

The children of Israel must have been sad, fearful, and discouraged, with the thoughts that God could judge them for their misdemeanors. But God interjected them through the prophet Nehemiah and asked them not to mourn or weep (verse 9). Instead, he asked them to go eat, drink, and rejoice. *For the joy of the Lord is your strength*, He says.

This lets us see how much the Lord is interested in our joy. Just as He encouraged the children of Israel to be joyful, He is doing the same to us. Isn't this the mindset behind the Pauline instruction to the Philippians? *Do not be anxious about anything...* (Philippians 4:6). God cares about us. He is more passionate about our success, health, and prosperity than we can ever be. And, sure enough, He is ever there to meet our needs. This is why he instructs us to be joyful always. Our expression of joy is, on our part, a demonstration of our faith in Him.

PRAYER

The joy of the Lord id my strength. I choose to be joyful irrespective of my challenges. As I walk in faith by being joyful, I overcome obstacles and live in line with God's will for me.

FURTHER STUDY

Romans 14:17. James 1:2

MY RESOLUTION

_____

_____

_____

Day 12: Being Joyful is Your Nature

Galatians 5:22

But the fruit of the Spirit is... joy

The text above contextually refers to the fruit of the recreated human spirit. Therefore, it relates to anyone who is born again or is a child of God. In other words, if you have received the gospel of Jesus Christ into your heart and have professed His lordship over your life, your spirit is now recreated in the character of Christ. If this is the case, you now have the fruits of the spirit, of which one of them is joy!

Joy can be said to be a state of ecstatic cheerfulness and comfort. It is, unlike happiness, often independent of the things happening around you. While your happiness can, for instance, spring from the fact that you've just gotten your dream job or that you've just acquired your dream home, joy comes from the inside. Your joy is a natural fruit of your recreated human spirit. It keeps you cheerful even during challenging times. It is an eternal state!

Now, when the Bible asks us to *"consider it pure joy"* when we face trials (James 1:2), it is because we have the capacity to do so—it is a function of our recreated human spirit. It's left to us simply yield to the spirit, choosing to consider the exciting realities of

God's promises to us in His word rather than our problems. Thus, we can be joyful always, irrespective of our trials and challenges.

PRAYER

Being joyful is native to me. I choose to be joyful irrespective of my external circumstances. I refuse to succumb to any element that would attempt to steal my joy, in Jesus' name.

FURTHER STUDY
Galatians 5:22-25. James 1:2-4

MY RESOLUTION

_____

_____

_____

Day 13: Change Your View

2Corinthians 4:18

So we fix our eyes not on what is seen, but on what is unseen, since what is seen is temporary, but what is unseen is eternal.

Looking back, I vividly recall several challenging situations I've been through. Surely, I've always pulled through every one of them. Not even the toughest of them came to stay. They all phased out, some faster than others. I am pretty certain that if you similarly take a quick appraisal of your life, you'll also find out how you've scaled through many challenging situations. Perhaps, some of these challenges threatened to become your "new normal." But, in the end, you went through them and came out of them.

Our faith and deliverance would be threatened when we focus on the challenges we're facing instead of the eternal blessings that we have in Christ. This is what the text above addresses. Focusing on our eternal salvation and the blessings that our union with the Lord provides us not only comforts us but also stirs up our joy! Hence, instead of focusing on the unpaid bills, for instance, you can focus and take advantage of the fact that you can fellowship with and hear from God.

A classic example of fixing our eyes on the eternal instead of the temporal is found in James' epistle: *consider it pure joy, brothers and sisters, whenever you face trials of different kinds, because you know that the testing of your faith produces perseverance...* (James 1:2-3). It's instructive how James encourages the church to rejoice in their persecution by fixing their eyes on the eternal fact that the trial of their faith would produce perseverance. The point here is that while their trouble(s) wouldn't last long, their blessings are eternal. It's the same with us.

PRAYER

I keep my eyes fixed on the eternal blessings that I have in Christ Jesus. I rejoice, because I am eternally blessed. I refuse to let temporal troubles cause me to be sad or despondent!

FURTHER STUDY

James 1:2-4. Romans 5:1-5

MY RESOLUTION

_____

_____

_____

Day 14: The Lord is Your Shepherd Indeed

Psalm 23:1-4

The LORD is my shepherd, I lack nothing. He makes me lie down in green pastures, he leads me beside quiet waters, he refreshes my soul. He guides me along the right paths for his name's sake. Even though I walk through the darkest valley, I will fear no evil, for you are with me; your rod and your staff, they comfort me.

The above scripture text is definitely one of the most popular texts of the Old Testament. It is a psalm of David that expresses the shepherd-like role God plays over us. He provides for us, protects us, guides us through the right parts, and so on. Many have become so familiar with this text of scripture that they no longer acknowledge the profound revelations of God in it. The truth is that He wants us to acknowledge these roles over our lives, just as David did.

Meditating on the shepherd-like role God plays over us would not only excite us, but it would also help us have the same confession David had: *...even though I walk through the darkest valley, I will fear no evil, for you are with me; your rod and your staff, they comfort me.* This ought to be the reality in our lives too. This is why God wants us to acknowledge and meditate on His word till it becomes natural to us.

Cultivate a daily practice of meditating on Psalm 23 and, of course, other promises in God's Word. Doing this often and often would not only build your faith but help you walk in the realities of God's word.

PRAYER

The Lord is my shepherd indeed. I belong to Him. I am His sheep. I am under His care. And I walk in sync with His leadership. Therefore, I would never be found wanting or stranded in life!

FURTHER STUDY
Psalm 91. Psalm 34:10

MY RESOLUTION

_____

_____

_____

Day 15: He Will Keep You from Stumbling

Jude 1:24

To him who is able to keep you from stumbling and to present you before his glorious presence without fault and with great joy.

To stumble in this context is to lose balance or fall in life's endeavors. This can mean backsliding in your faith or relationship with God or experiencing some sort of breakdown in any area of life. Now, the fear of stumbling is one with which most of us can relate. Many believers, for instance, fear losing their faith in God and the eternal damnation that may result from this. Some others may fear a mental or emotional breakdown that will cause them to function below their actual abilities.

We have a father that not only saves us and delivers us from trouble but also keeps us from stumbling or falling. This means He plays the role of a guarantor over our lives. He guarantees our salvation, sanity, health, etc. In expressing His role as the guarantor of our salvation, Jesus said, *I give them eternal life, and they shall never perish; no one will snatch them out of my hand* (John 10:28).

Our role is to stay in faith, trusting God to keep us from falling. He isn't waiting for us to fall so that He can punish us for not being careful enough or try to salvage the situation. No! He is that loving

Father that plays an active role in keeping us from falling. Remember that His love for us surpasses our love for our kids. He is the ideal Father who gives His all for us!

PRAYER
My heavenly Father keeps me from stumbling. I stay upright and firm always. I refuse to live an inconsistent and irregular life, in Jesus' name!

FURTHER STUDY
1John 2:1-2. John 10:27-30

MY RESOLUTION

_____

_____

_____

Day 16: His Angels Protect You

Psalm 91:11-12

For he will command his angels concerning you to guard you in all your ways; they will lift you up in their hands so that you will not strike your foot against a stone.

Angels are powerful spirit beings created by God. They serve to deliver God's messages to men, as intermediaries between God and man, and to carry out supernatural activities on earth in line with God's purposes. Angels are so mighty that they can do things that are impossible to man. Just an angel of God, for instance, delivered the children of Israel out of Egypt and their other enemies and led them on their way to the promised land (Exodus 14:19, 23:20, 32:34, 33:2).

God so much cares about our safety and wellbeing that He puts these powerful spirits in charge of us, His children. He assigns them to serve us supernaturally. *Are not all angels ministering spirits sent to serve those who will inherit salvation?* (Hebrews 1:14). Hence, they are always at our beck and call. The challenge here is that many believers aren't aware of the availability of angels to them.

We and everyone related to us can walk in supernatural provision and protection when we walk more in the consciousness that we have angels at our beck and call. We can activate the operation of angels with our words—speaking in consonance with God's promises for us in his word. Today, meditate on the fact that you have angels waiting on you and declare words concerning the circumstances in which you desire a change.

PRAYER
I am conscious of the ministry of angels around me. I take advantage of the angels waiting on me today, as I pray and declare faith-filled words, in Jesus' name.

FURTHER STUDY
Hebrews 1:4-7. Matthew 1:20-24

MY RESOLUTION

_____

_____

_____

Day 17: He wants to Help You Out

Romans 12:2

Do not conform to the pattern of this world, but be transformed by the renewing of your mind...

I remember, as a younger person, I struggled with a certain bad habit. I knew it was wrong, immoral, and bad for my Christian faith. But, no matter how much I tried to quit it, I constantly compromised somewhere along the line. Now, every time I compromised, I experienced an overwhelming sense of sin and guilt. Some of such times, I felt God was disappointed in me and was coming all out to punish me. But this was the wrong picture of God. He wasn't after me to punish me but to help me out.

My deliverance began when I discovered that the Father loves me unconditionally and was passionate about helping me out. That day, I became receptive to following His guidance for me. Then, He led me to the text above (Romans 12:2), where He says I can be "transformed" just by renewing the information in my mind. Not too long later, I came in contact with the scripture verse, *Do not be deceived: Evil company corrupts good habits* (1Corinthians 15:33 NKJV).

I gradually but consistently overcame my bad habit by totally separating myself from the wrong company (including the books

I read and TV programs I watched) and throwing myself into association with the right company. God helped me out. I allowed Him to do so, thanks to the correct information about Him.

Understand that God wants to help you out of your bad habits and addictions too. He wants to deliver you completely. God isn't condemning you. On the contrary, his arms are opened to welcome you if only you'll see Him for who He truly is: a loving Father who cares about you and would lay nothing to your charge.

PRAYER
Today, I am conscious of the fact that God cares for me and wants to help me out of my habits and addictions. I choose to give Him a chance today. I choose to renew my mind and stay away from the wrong company, in Jesus' name.

FURTHER STUDY
Colossians 3:8-10. 2Corinthians 6:14-17

MY RESOLUTION

_____

_____

_____

Day 18: True Rest is in Him

Matthew 11:28-29

Come unto me, all of you who are weary and burdened, and I will give you rest. Take my yoke upon you and learn from me, for I am gentle and humble in heart, and you will find rest for your souls.

Rest, in this context, means freedom from struggles or labor. It expresses the cessation of some difficult situations. Perhaps, you desire this form of rest in any area of life you have struggled with for a while. I'm glad to let you know that true and proper rest is found in Christ. Coming to Him is the starting point to your discovery of this rest.

You may say, *Well, I believe in Jesus Christ. I have come to Him already.* Perhaps, you're right. But that's not all you've got to do. The Lord Himself expounds on what it means to fully come to Him: *"Take my yoke upon you and learn of me."* This expression is particularly vital here. Taking His yoke upon us would mean doing His words and heeding His instructions; this is possible when we learn of Him. In learning of Him, we learn of His "yokes" and how to take them upon us.

True rest from your struggles and challenges is all in Christ! As you give heed to His word, prayers, fellowship, meditation, and consciously putting His word to work in your life, you will discover this true rest. Structure your daily schedules to accommodate time for prayers, study, meditation, etc. In the end, you'll be glad you did.

I have come to true rest in Christ. I choose to walk in this true rest always. Hence, I have ceased from my struggles and fears, in Jesus' name.

FURTHER STUDY
Hebrews 4:1-3. John 14:6

MY RESOLUTION

_____

_____

_____

Day 19: His Grace is Sufficient for You

2Corinthians 12:9

But he said unto me, "My grace is sufficient for you, for my strength is made perfect in weakness." Therefore I will boast all the more gladly about my weakness, so that Christ's power may rest on me.

Have you ever felt like you are at your wit's end? Have you tried all you know to do to become a better version of yourself and still failed? Perhaps, you have repeatedly failed in your constant attempts to become a better parent, child, teacher, neighbor, mentor, staff, citizen, etc. Well, you don't have to depend on your human efforts. God's grace is sufficient for you. His strength is reliable to cover up for your weakness.

Our human strength and ability aren't always sufficient enough to address our challenges. *...It is not by strength that one prevails* (1Samuel 2:9). This is where the grace of God comes in! It takes over at the boundaries of our human effort. Our responsibility is to acknowledge our weaknesses and trust God for His grace over our circumstances.

Taking advantage of God's grace means openly acknowledging our limitations while also expressing our trust in the grace of God. You can practice this by, for instance, saying: *My abilities are limited here, but I am sure the grace of God is sufficient for me.* You can cultivate this expression into your daily language. Instead of expressing despair and hopelessness, you can express your trust in the grace of God to cover up for your weakness. Surely, somehow, His grace would stand in where your abilities fail.

PRAYER
I take advantage of the grace of God over my affairs today. I acknowledge that His grace is sufficient for me and perfect in my weakness.

FURTHER STUDY
2Timothy 2:1. 2Corinthians 9:8

MY RESOLUTION

_____

_____

_____

Day 20: You Can Be Strong Again

Isaiah 40:31 (NKJV)

But those who wait on the Lord shall renew their strength. They shall mount up with wings like eagles, they shall run and not be weary, they shall walk and not faint.

Getting tired after engaging in any laborious work or task is a norm in nature. This is where the need for rest (and food) comes in. Just as our bodies are naturally wired to constantly require food and rest to renew our energy levels, our Spirits need "waiting on the Lord" to restore our inward strength and vitality. Given this, a Spiritual life without a culture of constantly waiting on the Lord is unhealthy.

The story of Elijah presents some imagery of the need for "waiting on the Lord." Queen Jezebel had sent a message to him that she would have him killed (1Kings 19:2). Elijah feared for his life and fled into the wilderness, scared, frustrated, depressed, and suicidal. But, while he slept in the wilderness, God sent an angel to feed him with baked bread twice. The Bible records that Elijah was *…strengthened by the food, he traveled forty days and forty nights until he reached Horeb, the mountain of God* (verse 8)

Waiting on the Lord is our surest way to renewing our strength and reversing our confusion, lethargy, and discouragement. As the word "wait on" implies, to wait on the Lord means to devote time to be with Him. It means earmarking and devoting a reasonable amount of time to fellowship with the Lord. This can be in the form of prayers, worship, and study. It can also be in the form of meditation or a "quiet time" to be sensitive to His leading in your heart.

PRAYER
I choose to wait upon the Lord today and always. I refuse to be distracted from my devotion to Him. I affirm that I am unwaveringly committed to my consecrated times of fellowship with God.

FURTHER STUDY
Acts 20:38. Psalm 130:5-8

MY RESOLUTION

_____

_____

_____

Day 21: Don't be Afraid; Just Believe

Luke 8:50

Hearing this, Jesus said to Jairus, "Don't be afraid; just believe...."

The text above is from an inspiring story from the gospel account of Luke. The man, Jairus, had come to plead with Jesus to go with him to his home to heal his sick daughter. Jesus obliged him. But, on the way, a sick woman received her healing by sneaking through the crowds that thronged Jesus to touch the edge of the cloak He was wearing. Jesus supernaturally realized this and called for the woman. She then narrated her ordeal and the miracle she had just received. Jesus then blessed her.

Jesus was still speaking with the woman when someone came from Jairus' house and said, *Your daughter is dead... Don't bother the teacher anymore* (Luke 8:49). Jesus heard this and immediately told Jairus, *Don't be afraid; just believe* (verse 50). The negative information could rob Jairus of his faith. This was the reason for Jesus' sharp interjection. Jairus' daughter was raised back to life at the end of the day!

Just as Jesus said to Jairus, "don't be afraid, just believe," He is saying the same to us today. He knows that there are lots of contrary information around with the capacity to hurt our faith. Hence, He is interjecting our minds, imploring us just to believe.

Just as it was with Jairus, the contrary information is only a mirage. They have no substance. God's power can switch them if only you dare to believe!

PRAYER

I walk in faith always. I refuse to let fear rob me of the miracles that are in store for me. By faith, I walk in the supernatural in all facet of my life, in Jesus' name!

FURTHER STUDY

Matthew 8:13. Romans 4:3-5.

MY RESOLUTION

_____

_____

_____

Day 22: You Can Practice Joyfulness

Ephesians 5:18-19

Do not get drunk on wine, which leads to debauchery. Instead, be filled with the Spirit, speaking to one another with psalms, hymns, and songs from the Spirit. Sing and make music in your heart to the Lord.

As you already learned on Day 12, being joyful is natural to you. This means you can straight-up practice being joyful. The above text lucidly shows us how to do this—interacting with one another in joyful psalms, hymns, and songs from your Spirit. *How do I practice this when alone (with no one around with whom I could interact)?* The answer to this also features in the same scripture: *"sing and make music in your heart to the Lord."*

The psalmist understood the art of practicing joyfulness when he said: *I will be glad and rejoice in you; I will sing the praises of your name, O Most High* (Psalm 9:2). Isn't this something you and I can practice in our individual capacities? We can choose to shed off unpleasant feelings and stir-up joy from within by practicing joyfulness this way.

The epistle to the church at Philippi instructs Christians *to rejoice in the Lord always* (Philippians 4:4). This lets us see that it is a core Christian culture to practice joyfulness. We are instructed to do it constantly because we can, and it is our nature to do so. This means, irrespective of what happens or how we feel, we can always practice joyfulness.

PRAYER

I refuse to give in to the flesh. I refuse to allow external circumstances take away my joy. I practice joyfulness today and always, in Jesus' name.

FURTHER STUDY

Philippians 3:3. 1Peter 4:13

MY RESOLUTION

_____

_____

_____

Day 23: Use Your Faith

2Corinthians 5:7

For we live by faith, not by sight

It is usual for us as humans to be drawn towards the things that we see. The world wires us to seek physical proof before accepting something to be reality. But this isn't the same approach with spiritual things. To walk in spiritual realities or to operate in the supernatural, we have to exercise our faith to believe in the unseen with our hearts. Our faith in God, for instance, isn't because we see Him with our optical eyes but an exercise of our faith.

Living by faith opposes living by sight directly. To live by faith means believing without having to see. Our Lord, Jesus Christ, expressed this fact in His words: ...if you believe, you will see... (John 11:40). To live by sight means having to see before believing—to live by sensory experience.

While certain aspects of our lives may require the need for physical verification, we aren't expected to build our lives on our sensory experience but faith in God. Now, faith in God means faith in His word. It means holding on to the promises of God's word whether or not it conforms to our sensory experience. Praying and believing you'll get an answer, for instance, is an act of faith rather than sight.

Living by faith means trusting in God's promises for you. It means taking your attention off your unfavorable realities and, instead, keeping your gaze on God's word to you. You can walk in faith today by meditating and thinking on His love for you and His power available to and in you instead of the complex challenges and daunting tasks before you.

PRAYER

I live by faith and not by sight. I stay firmly attentive to God's word and promises for me. I do and practice His word without doubting!

FURTHER STUDY

Hebrews 10:38. 2Corinthians 4:17-18

MY RESOLUTION

_____

_____

_____

Day 24: His Compassions Never Fail

Lamentations 3:22-23

Because of the LORD's great love, we are not consumed, for his compassions never fail. They are new every morning; great is thy faithfulness.

Relationships are vital to us as humans. Our interaction with others contributes to our humanness and shapes our senses of purpose and fulfillment. However, our relationships have limitations. One of these limitations is our tendency to be easily pissed by continual error or unfaithfulness on the other person's part. If, for instance, a friend has a habit of constantly pissing you off and returning with an apology, it's only human not to value such a friendship. But God's not that way!

As the opening text insinuates, it is by God's "great love" that we are not consumed. His compassions never fail and are renewed every morning. In other words, God is not that friend that is pissed off by our unfaithfulness. While we may be unable to tolerate an unfaithful friend for long, God can tolerate our disloyalty continually.

God's faithfulness is so great that it can cause us to repent of our unfaithfulness. The epistle to the church at Rome puts this fact very clearly: *Or do you show contempt for the riches of his kindness, forbearance, and patience, not realizing that God's kindness is intended to lead you to repentance?* (Romans 2:4).

The Father is ever kind, gracious, and compassionate towards you. His relationship with you is far different from your relationship with other men. Your failures may cause other men to flee from you. But God remains unconditionally committed to you. He sees your heart; He knows how much you are trying to be the best version of yourself, and He is willing to help you. So get to Him in fellowship today, and savor your relationship with Him.

PRAYER

Dear Father, I recognize and appreciate your unconditional love for me. Thank you for the privilege to fellowship with you despite my faults. I take advantage of your relationship with me today and always. I choose to be transformed by it, in Jesus' name!

FURTHER STUDY

2Peter 3:9. Romans 8:35-39

MY RESOLUTION

_____

_____

_____

Day 25: Fear No Evil

Psalm 23:4

Even though I walk through the darkest valley, I will fear no evil, for you are with me; your rod and your staff, they comfort me.

In our world today, we are surrounded by lots of information intended to ignite fear and panic. But we need to remember that fear is the opposite of faith in God. To be fearful means to be lacking confidence in the love of God for you, His concern for you, or in His ability to save or provide for you.

We can take a cue from David's resolve in the opening text above. He states that he trusts that God is with him even though he walks through the toughest of situations! We can do the same. We can do this by choosing not to dwell on negative information around us but to meditate on God's power, unwavering love, and mercy that is available to us. Doing this, in itself, would be an act of faith.

The negative news about the pandemic, crashing economy, crises, rumors of unpleasant laws, etc., should have nothing on us. This is because God's power can reverse any harmful situation or circumstance for our good. He can make a way where there seems to be none! Instead of fretting, you can choose to take your requests to God in prayer, trusting that He would hear you. You can walk in the confidence that, when you pray, you get answers!

PRAYER

Today, I trust in God's power at work in me to reverse all unfavorable circumstances through prayer. With my prayers, I can effect desired changes in any part of the world. I walk continually in faith and not in fear, in Jesus' name.

FURTHER STUDY
Hebrews 10:22-23. 1Peter 5:-9

MY RESOLUTION

_____

_____

_____

Day 26: Kill Fear with Words of Faith

Proverbs 18:20-21

From the fruit of their mouth, a person's stomach is filled; with the harvest of their lips they are satisfied. The tongue has the power of life and death, and those who love it will eat its fruit.

A lot of times, we tend to ignore the power of words. This, of course, can owe to a lack of sufficient knowledge on the part of many. But for many other believers who have some scriptural understanding of the power of our words, we are often too given to our emotions that we let them determine what we say. The spiritual consequences of these may be unfavorable. Sometimes, our anxieties, lusts, failures can owe to our misuse of words.

The words we speak are so powerful that they can affect our lives and determine our relationships with others. Studies, for instance, have shown that the words we speak to or about ourselves can affect us cognitively, thus influencing our moods, how we do what we do, and how we relate with others. The epistle of Peter instructs on the need to be careful with our words: *For whoever would love life and see good days must keep their tongue from evil...* (1Peter 3:19).

We can choose to use our words to dispel doubts, fear, depression, and any unwanted feeling. Instead of lamenting about any unfavorable or undesirable situation, for instance, you can speak words of faith concerning it, declaring the realities you desire about it. If you're going through some financial difficulty, say, *in the name of Jesus, my needs are met supernaturally* (Philippians 4:13). If it's confusion concerning any area of your life, say, in the name of Jesus, *I refuse to be stranded. I walk in God's supernatural leading* (Psalm 23: 2-3, Romans 8:14).

PRAYERS

I refuse to let my emotions determine my use of words. I speak in consonance with God's plans for me. I speak in line with God's word for me. I do not use words wrongly, in Jesus' name.

FURTHER STUDY
Proverbs 15:4. Ephesians 4:29

MY RESOLUTION

_____

_____

_____

Day 27: Don't Look at the Wind

Matthew 14:30-31

But when he saw the wind, he was afraid and, beginning to sink, cried out, "Lord, save me!" Immediately Jesus reached out his hand and caught him. "You of little faith," he said, "why did you doubt?"

The opening text is taken from a famous story in the gospel account of Matthew. The disciples of Jesus were aboard a boat on the sea. Now, Jesus wasn't with them; He had sent them ahead of Him in the boat while He stayed behind to pray (Matthew 14:22-23).

While the disciples were still on the journey, they saw Jesus walking on the lake towards them and thought it was a ghost. But Jesus interjected them, "It is I" (verse 24-27). *"Lord, if it's you,"* Peter replied, tell me to come to you on the water" (verse 28). "Come," Jesus answered. So Peter got off the boat and began to walk up to Jesus on the lake (verse 29)!

Sometimes, in reading this story in scripture, we tend not to recognize that Peter walked on water. It wasn't Jesus alone who walked on water that night. Peter did too. Well, something happened along the line that tainted his miracle. He looked at the wind! When he saw the wind, he got scared and began to sink (verse 30). The problem started the moment he looked at the wind.

Peter's faith had been stirred from Jesus' word for him to "come." He then got off the boat into the lake, looking at Jesus. As long as he looked at Jesus, he walked on water. The sinking began the moment he took his gaze of Jesus. Isn't this just instructive!

Just like Peter, we can "walk on water" too. This means we can experience the miraculous and supernatural in our lives as long as we keep our gaze on Jesus and our minds on His word. We have to avoid looking at the contrary narratives around us. Instead, we've got to stay focused on His word.

PRAYER
My gaze is on Jesus Christ. I keep the word of God in my heart and refuse to consider contrary thoughts and opinions. I walk in the supernatural in Jesus' name!

FURTHER STUDY
Ecclesiastes 11:4. Jonah 2:8.

MY RESOLUTION

_____

_____

_____

Day 28: Practice Affirmation

Hebrews 13:5-6

Keep your lives free from the love of money and be content with what you have, because God has said, "Never will I leave you; never will I forsake you." So we say with confidence, "The Lord is my helper; I will not be afraid...

Affirmation means saying or declaring something in agreement with something or someone else. In this case, it is the declaration of God's word, a confession, or an assertion of our beliefs and convictions from God's word. The practice of affirmation is so essential to our lives such that it is the principle with which we received salvation in the first place. Romans 10:9 says, *if you declare with your mouth, "Jesus is Lord," and believe in your* heart *that God raised him from the dead, you shall be saved.*

Everything God has declared concerning us in His words may not become real to us until we affirm them. This means those great promises in God's word concerning our success, prosperity, peace, etc., may remain theoretical to us until we practice affirming them over our lives, our world, and the circumstances concerning us.

It is essential to practice affirmation when we pray. It is a very effective way to "ask" according to God's will. The epistle of John lets us know that *if we ask anything according to his will, he hears us* (John 5:14). Since affirmation entails simply declaring the realities of God's word over our lives, it is a way to pray in accordance with God's word (which is his will).

PRAYER

Henceforth, I consciously pray and affirm the truths of God's Word in faith. I embrace the culture of regularly directing the course of my life through faith-filled affirmations, in Jesus' name!

FURTHER STUDY

Mark 11:23-24. Romans 10:7-10

MY RESOLUTION

_____

_____

_____

Day 29: You Have Peace with God

Romans 5:1

Therefore, since we have been justified by faith, we have peace with God through our Lord Jesus Christ.

In a world that is filled with hostility, tribulation, war, conflict, etc., what every human's soul yearns for is peace. We seek peace in the world, particularly in relation to other persons. Now, while this is great, nothing comes close to being at peace with God. Being at peace with God is to be at peace in our innermost being. It is a state of tranquility on the inside. This is what God offers us in Jesus Christ. We got this simply by our faith in the gospel of Jesus Christ.

The peace that we have with God means there is no need to be afraid that, one day, He will punish us for our wrongs. It means He would never do anything to hurt us. This peace means, irrespective of our faults and imperfections, God still loves us and would never deny or fail us. Also, this peace with God means we can pray to and communicate with Him and expect answers!

The epistle to the church at Ephesus explains this peace lucidly: *But now in Christ Jesus, you who once were far away have been brought near by the blood of Christ. For he himself is our peace...* (Ephesians 2:13-14). By our faith in Christ Jesus, we are at peace with God. Therefore, we've got absolutely nothing to be scared of as far as our relationship with God is concerned. We are simply at peace with Him.

PRAYER

Jesus Christ is my peace. By my faith in Christ, I have eternal peace with God. I am in an irrevocable union with Him. I live my life with a consciousness of this union, producing relevant fruits, in Jesus' name!

FURTHER STUDY
Romans 5:8-21. Ephesians 2:1-22.

MY RESOLUTION

_____

_____

_____

Day 30: Your Prayers are Powerful and Effective

James 5:16

...The prayer of a righteous person is powerful and effective

Perhaps, upon reading the above scripture text, you asked yourself a question, *Am I righteous?* If I am permitted to respond to this question, I would ask, *do you have faith in the gospel of Jesus Christ?* This is because no one can be righteous by their efforts. The scriptures let us see that *...all have sinned and have come short of the glory of God* (Romans 3:23).

Given the inability of a man to attain righteousness by his works or efforts, God sent Jesus Christ to the world to be the propitiation for our sins. Hence, righteousness comes by faith in His works. The book of Romans puts it this way: *...all are justified freely by his grace through redemption that came by Jesus Christ. God presented Christ as a sacrifice of atonement through the shedding of his blood...* (Romans 3:24-25). Hence, *righteousness is given through faith in Jesus Christ to all who believe* (Romans 3:22).

If you believe in the gospel of Jesus Christ, you are the righteous person being referred to in the opening text (James 5:16). Therefore, your prayers are powerful and effective. When you go to God in prayers, you can be sure to get the answer you desire.

Be excited to take your situations and circumstances to God in prayers, knowing you are a righteous person, and God is ever-ready to answer them. Instead of allowing fear, rejection, or depression to take hold of your mind, take solace in the fact that you are righteous and God is ever-willing to grant you audience.

PRAYER

My prayers are powerful and effective. I believe that every time I pray, I receive answers. Today and always, as I pray for myself, my loved ones, and for the will of God on earth, I do so in faith that my prayers produce results.

FURTHER STUDY

Romans 5:1-21. James 5:14-18

MY RESOLUTION

_____

_____

_____

About The Author

Chloe Schaffer is a Christian author, speaker, wife, and mother. She is married to a Christian missionary to Africa and has served on several such missions where they have pioneered several churches. Her passion is to take the good news of Christ's work of redemption to all classes of people worldwide. She is primarily resident in Oregon, USA, where she lives with her family when she isn't on the field with her husband.

Printed in the USA
CPSIA information can be obtained
at www.ICGtesting.com
CBHW040239231024
16239CB00063B/1060